COLOUR AND LEARN
ABOUT GOD

GOD HAS POWER

God has power

He made the whole world. "In the beginning God created the heavens and the earth." Genesis 1:1

God

— — —

world

— — — — —

created

— — — — — — —

Page 2 Key words:

God

world

created

God has power

He makes the sun rise in the morning and set in the evening."God makes his sun rise on the evil and the good. God sends rain on the righteous and the unrighteous." Matthew 5:45

sun

— — —

morning

— — — — — — —

evening

— — — — — — —

Go over the words you have learnt so far:

God
world
created
sun
morning
evening

God has power

He can make the wind blow very hard. He can make the wind blow gently. "Jesus got up and rebuked the wind and the raging waters... and all was calm." Luke 8:24

wind

— — — —

blow

— — — —

calm

— — — —

Go over the words you have learnt so far:

God	wind
world	blow
created	calm
sun	
morning	
evening	

God has power

He can make the sea rough and stormy. He can make the sea smooth and calm. "The men were amazed and asked, what kind of man is this? Even the winds and the waves obey him." Matthew 8:27

sea

— — —

stormy

— — — — — —

obey

— — — —

Go over the words you have learnt so far:

God	wind
world	blow
created	calm
sun	sea
morning	stormy
evening	obey

God has power

He made all the animals. Some are big and some are small. "And God said, 'Let the land produce living creatures that move along the ground, and wild animals.'" Genesis 1:24

animals

— — — — — — —

big

— — —

small

— — — — —

Page 10 Key words:

animals

big

small

Go over the words you have learnt so far:

God	wind	animals
world	blow	big
created	calm	small
sun	sea	
morning	stormy	
evening	obey	

God has power

He gives us life and breath. He has power to forgive us when we do wrong. "The Son of Man has authority on earth to forgive sins." Matthew 9:6

life

— — — —

forgive

— — — — — — —

sins

— — — —

Page 12 Key words:

life

forgive

sins

Go over the words you have learnt so far:

God	wind	animals
world	blow	big
created	calm	small
sun	sea	life
morning	stormy	forgive
evening	obey	sins

These are all the words that you have learnt in this book. Try and fit them into the gaps in the following story to see how well you have learnt them.

	morning	sea	small
God	evening	stormy	life
world	wind	obey	forgive
created	blow	animals	sins
sun	calm	big	

Did you know that ___ __ __ made the whole __ __ __ __ __?

He __ __ __ __ __ __ __it. God is so powerful that he created

everyone and everything. He made the __ __ __ to shine in the

__ __ __ __ __ __ __. We should thank him for this. He made

the moon to shine in the __ __ __ __ __ __ __. We should thank

him for this. God has power over everything. He can make the

__ __ __ __   __ __ __ __ strongly. God is so powerful that he

can make the weather __ __ __ __.

God is so powerful that even when the __ __ __ becomes wild

and __ __ __ __ __ __ it will become quiet and __ __ __ __

God. __ __ __ __ __ __ __ are in God's control. __ __ __

animals and __ __ __ __ __ animals obey him. We should thank

God for the__ __ __ __ that he has given us. He is so powerful he

can even __ __ __ __ __ __ __ us our __ __ __ __.